TIMOTHY YOUNG

Understanding Your
OFFSHORE
INJURY

··

Insider Tips from a Jones Act Attorney
That Could Protect You & Your Family

Timothy Young, **The Young Firm**
www.JonesActLaw.com

UNDERSTANDING YOUR OFFSHORE INJURY

Copyright © 2009, Second Edition Copyright © 2013 Timothy Young

All rights reserved. No part of this book may be used or reproduced in any manner whatsoever without written permission of the author.

Printed in the United States of America

ISBN-13: 978-1491209158
ISBN-10: 1491209151

TIMOTHY YOUNG

Disclaimer: This book is meant for informational purposes only. The legal statutes mentioned in this book were current as of the publication date, however, we cannot guarantee that these statutes have remained the same since the publication date. The information contained herein is not intended, and should not be taken, as legal advice. You are advised to contact a maritime attorney for counsel on particular issues and concerns. Additionally, your use or request of our materials does not constitute as an attorney-client relationship between you and The Young Firm.

WHAT COULD I POSSIBLY KNOW ABOUT YOU?

For more than 20 years I've represented injured maritime workers.

I've sat in your homes, eaten dinner and supper with you and your families as we talked about your options and concerns.

You told me about the 'company' doctors you'd seen and how they refused to take care of you. The company rep went with you each time and it always made you a little uncomfortable.

You told me how you were pressured into giving a recorded statement. And how more than anything you simply wanted to go back to the job you loved.

You also told me about the fear and worry you had when you made the leap to file a claim. You talked about the guys you used to work with, and how they were like family to you. It didn't matter that it was actually the company lawyers and claims people calling the shots now, not your crew. You still felt there was a place for you out there.

Before the other side would grill you, you and I'd go over everything. Afterwards, almost in awe, you'd say how spot on I had been predicting their questions. (Those company lawyers always ask the same things).

You'd finally go to the doctor like you needed. And you didn't have to scrape by anymore on the few measly hundred dollars a month the company gave you.

We made sure we demanded a fair settlement for you. And if we didn't get it, we went to court to fight for it.

This is what I know about you: You worked hard, invested in your future with a great career, and now you find yourself in a place where you're nervous, uncertain and, frankly, a little scared.

You're nervous about making a bad decision. Uncertain about which road to take. Scared because you feel like it is you against 'them' and they're big and intimidating.

But you may be thinking, Who is this guy? What does he know?

I have a family just like you. I work very hard at my career and love what I do, just like you did before your injury. I have people who work for me and I listen to what's important to them and their *families.*

I have stood in front of many juries and put them in your shoes, told them your story and how you never wanted to end up in a courtroom.

I give out books to educate people and other lawyers hire me to help them with their maritime cases. I'm like the heart surgeon of attorneys; I only focus on one thing: maritime cases.

They're that important to your future. They can change your life forever, and that's more than enough reason for me to give it my all, to focus all my energies on your case and cases just like yours.

I like a challenge; I like standing up to company lawyers who intimidate, bully and hide behind a bunch of complicated laws. I get furious when they try to make you look like a liar or a cheat after you worked so hard for them.

More than anything, I work hard so I can make a difference to our clients. I want to educate you and create options for you. I want to play a significant role in helping you to create a much better future for you than you would've had if we'd never met.

I know all this doesn't have much to do with

the law, but it has everything to do with you. The situation you are in today is about you. Not me or my past clients or the high-dollar cases we have won.

So if you have questions about your situation and where you can go from here, call me now. The longer you wait to take action, the worse your situation may get.

Sincerely,
Tim Young

TABLE OF CONTENTS

FAQS..12
Should I Go Back to Work ASAP?..........12
Should I Settle on My Own?......................14
Isn't There a Blacklist?.....................15
Will My Advances Be Cut Off?..................16
How Much Will I Get for My Injury?....18
How Long Will My Case Take?..................19

THE LAW UNLOCKED..........21
MARITIME LAW & POWER......21
JONES ACT HIDDEN SECRETS...23
Why Is the Jones Act Important?..............24
ARE YOU A SEAMAN?......................25
When Does the Jones Act Apply?............25
ARE YOU BEING KEPT SAFE?........29
What's Considered "Unsafe"?...................30
5 Tactics Your Company Will Use..............35
COMMON MYTHS DEBUNKED...39
They Can't Make You Sign.....................39
Your Injury, Your Doctor of Choice..............41
Their Doctor, Their Mistake....................43

ENOUGH'S ENOUGH............45
LET THE LAW FIGHT FOR YOU..49
TYPES OF COMPENSATION.........49
    Pain & Suffering..49
    Medical Expenses.......................................50
    Loss of Wages..50
    Loss of Fringe Benefits...............................51
MAKING THE LEAP........................53
    How Soon Should You Hire a Lawyer?......53
    Finding the Right Person for the Job........55
    5 Must-Have Qualities................................57
FILING A MARITIME CLAIM......61
    Negligence..62
    Unseaworthiness..64
    Damages...64
    Punitive Damages......................................65
    Maintenance and Cure..............................65

MEDICAL INFO......................69
COMMON MEDICAL TESTS.........69

ABOUT THIS BOOK

Understanding your rights is the first step to protecting yourself. You rely upon your employers as well as your coworkers for your day-to-day safety. Your company should follow the law and give you a safe place to work, because you work in very dangerous environments. If you have been injured while working offshore on a platform or vessel, it is critical that you are familiar with your rights. Handling your injury is about more than taking care of your body; it is about taking care of you and your family's future.

This maritime law guide will help you understand your basic maritime and Jones Act rights. Please understand that maritime law and the Jones Act law are very complicated. Our office has handled maritime claims for more than fifty years and we limit our practice to helping individuals injured on oil rigs and vessels.

This guide is set up into four parts: The Basics, Filing a Claim, FAQs, and Medical Info. Each of these parts have subsections expanding on different concepts. At the end of major subsections are "Main Points" that help summarize the ideas expressed.

There are also "Insider Insight" boxes scattered throughout the book that highlight important issues that you should pay attention to.

In addition to the "Insider Insights" are the "Insider Tip" boxes which give you specific actions you can take to improve your situation now. These are meant to be simple steps that will either further educate you about your situation or will give you suggestions on how you can prevent further issues from popping up down the road.

Lastly, there are definitions of common terms at the bottom of pages along with an index at the back of the book that points to specific pages where those terms are discussed.

This guide is meant only as an introduction to maritime and Jones Act law. Some of the statements herein may not apply to your specific case. If you have any questions after reading this guide, please be sure to phone our office so that we can discuss your questions in detail.

With that said, we congratulate you on taking the time and effort to educate yourself on your basic day-to-day rights while working offshore or on a vessel! With the information in this guide, you will have a more comprehensive understanding of how you should be treated while working offshore.

FAQS

QUICK & DIRECT ANSWERS TO YOUR BURNING QUESTIONS

Should I Go Back to Work ASAP?

You should not attempt to return to work unless your injury was *very* minor and your personal doctor has approved the decision. You must be 100% positive that you have *fully* recovered from your injury. Even if the pain is tolerable and you can perform most of your duties, it would be wise to wait until your doctor says you're fit to work. Many workers insist that they want to return to work immediately after their injury because they need to continue supporting their families.

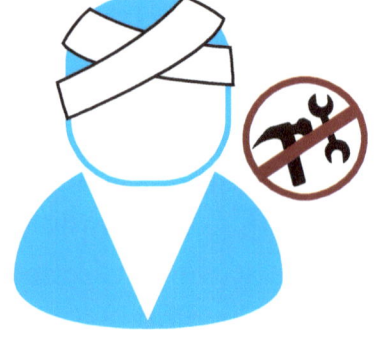

This is "penny wise but pound foolish" as they say. Some of these workers will receive treatment from company-chosen doctors who immediately release them to "attempt" to return to work following their injury. Very often this can be a critical mistake to your future.

If your injury becomes aggravated or worsened after you attempt to return to work, very often the company will then claim that you are responsible for making your injury worse. Even though the doctor may have returned you to work, the focus of your claim will then become if you made your injury worse after you returned to work. You will be faced with a situation of having to prove that you did not seriously aggravate or worsen your condition when you attempted to return to work.

Additionally, many companies will claim after you return to work that "you were perfectly fine while at work." In other words your company may be watching you after you return to work and even if you later claim that your condition continued to bother you, your company may claim that you were perfectly fine after you returned to work.

Finally, once you return to work your company will very often refuse to provide you with any further medical treatment. Your company will argue that since you were able to return to work, you no longer need medical treatment. Overall, returning to work too quickly before you have fully recovered from your injury can not only ruin your maritime injury claim if you file one but can also seriously worsen your injury.

Should I Settle On My Own?

Many offshore workers ask if they should meet alone with the company or the company's insurance representative to discuss settlement with the company, before the worker speaks with or hires an attorney. In almost all cases this is a *horrible* mistake.

First, the company typically will not make a firm offer to you. Instead the company will repeatedly ask "how much" you would like to settle the claim for. No matter what figure you give to the company or the insurance representative, the company or insurance representative will offer significantly less. Sometimes the injured employee has no idea the value of his claim if he has not yet talked to a maritime lawyer.

You may believe $10,000, $15,000, or even $20,000 is a fair amount for the injury you've incurred, but your medical bills could come out to three times that amount and so your case could potentially be worth much more. Your company's objective is to pay as little as possible; yours should be to look after your injury and your future.

More importantly, very often injured maritime workers will try to settle their claims so that they can obtain money to receive further medical treatment. If there is any need whatsoever for further medical treatment, it is critical that you *do not* settle your claim until all necessary medical treatment has been performed. Most company doctors will not perform expensive medical testing to fully discover any possible injury. You simply cannot settle your maritime claim until an independent, trustworthy doctor has performed all such testing. It would be like trying to buy a car without test driving the car, or even seeing the car beforehand. You would simply be guessing at the value.

Isn't There a Blacklist?

The "blacklist" was a rumor started many years ago by offshore companies in an effort to scare employees from filing suit. Our office has handled claims for several individuals who have successfully returned to work offshore following the resolution of their injury claims.

When you apply for employment in the future after your maritime injury, it is critical that you are honest about your past injury and the medical treatment that you have received. However, companies should not ask if you have ever filed suit in the past. If such question is on your application, you are under *no* legal obligation to answer such question.

Will My Advances Be Cut Off?

Many maritime companies provide employees with monthly payments that the company characterizes as "advances." While it is true that most companies will terminate these "advancements" if you file suit, in almost all cases you will have other means of financial support which can be used in such situations. If you have any short or long-term disability insurance, you can apply for and typically receive such benefits during your case. Additionally, some state laws allow attorneys to advance clients living expenses while their suits are being prosecuted. Finally, if the company has characterized your monthly living expenses as "advances," a good maritime lawyer will argue that such payments should have been included under your "maintenance" payment. It is always best to think *long term* in regards to your maritime injury rather than month to month. You should be concerned about your future over the next three to five years and not your monthly expenses over the next three to five months.

The Company Doctor Won't Treat Me! What Should I Do?

If you are receiving medical treatment from a company chosen doctor, very often the doctor will not immediately perform medical testing to fully diagnose the nature and extent of your injuries. Today basic medi cal testing should include MRIs as well as nerve conduction studies. An MRI may be performed on your neck, shoulder, back, knees, ankles and other parts of your body. The MRI test shows soft tissue and ligament damages that are not seen on a plain film X-ray. If the company chosen doctor is refusing to perform basic medical testing including MRIs, you should seek medical treatment elsewhere from a local physician you know and trust.

Unfortunately, many companies have little desire to pay for medical testing which could prove the seriousness of your injury. Very often when the company doctor delays or refuses to perform basic medical testing, it is the first sign that the company is fighting your case.

> ¤ **Soft tissue**- Soft tissue injuries are those related to the tendons, ligaments, connective tissue, skin, fat, muscles, nerves, and blood vessels, but not bone.

How Much Will I Get for My Injury?

Every case must be evaluated on the facts of the case. There are a few basic, important factors that generally determine the difference between a relatively small valued case and a higher valued case. One of these factors is the amount of money you previously earned as opposed to how much you'll be earning after your injury.

If you have suffered an injury which prevents you from returning to heavy manual labor and you previously earned significant wages working offshore or performing heavy manual labor for a maritime company, in all likelihood you will have a significant loss of future wage claim.

> **Estimating the Value of Your Jones Act Case**
>
> $ Previous Income
> − Income after injury
> ―――――――――――
> Amount of lost wages

Most high-dollar Jones Act and maritime injury claims involve significant loss of wage claims in addition to pain and suffering damages and medical expenses.

One way to estimate the value of your Jones Act claim is to ask how much money you will earn returning to limited or light duty work following your maritime injury. You will then need to compare this amount of income with what you were earning offshore or on the water.

How Long Will My Case Take?

Maritime injury cases are not quick, simple cases. In a typical "soft tissue" car accident case, a paralegal or legal staff member will negotiate a fast settlement of a few thousand dollars for you with an insurance company adjuster.

Your maritime injury case is much more serious and complicated. Your case will be handled by attorneys. Typically if you have suffered a serious injury, especially injuries which have required surgery, you may be seeking hundreds of thousands of dollars, if not more.

Maritime companies and their insurance companies simply do not pay settlements of this amount without fully investigating and attempting to fight your claim. This process takes at least a few months even for smaller claims, and most serious maritime claims can take 12 to 14 months to resolve.

The time period depends greatly upon the court

where your suit has been filed. Some courts are much quicker than others. However, you will usually have an idea of the value of your case within a few months of filing suit.

Main Points:

1. You should not attempt to return to work unless you are completely healed.
2. It is *not* in your best interest to settle your case on your own. Settling on your own could mean that you miss out on hundreds of thousands of dollars that are rightfully yours.
3. There is no such thing as a blacklist. We have had several clients return to work offshore after their injury. No company should ever ask you if you filed suit in the past.
4. Many times companies will stop "advancements" once you hire an attorney. However, there are several ways to supplement this lost income.
5. If the company doctor is refusing to give you proper testing, you should seek your own doctor.
6. Cases can take anywhere from three to 14 months, but it all depends on your unique situation.
7. Your case could be worth hundreds of thousands of dollars depending on the facts of your situation.

TIMOTHY YOUNG

THE LAW UNLOCKED
THE POWER OF MARITIME LAW

General maritime law (also known informally as "maritime law") applies to any injury or claim that occurs on "navigable" water. The definition of navigable water certainly includes the Mississippi River as well as the Gulf of Mexico. Many times it is not difficult to determine if a body of water is "navigable" for purposes of maritime law. It is also important to determine whether any land-based laws apply to your injury.

Although fixed platforms in the Gulf of Mexico are sitting on "navigable water," generally, maritime law *does not* apply to injuries and accidents which occur on the fixed platform. Instead, the law of the state where the platform is located will usually apply to such situations. For example, if a worker is injured while working on a fixed platform off of the coast of Louisiana, and

> ¤ **General maritime law**- a type of law that applies to any injury that occurs on navigable water.
> ¤ **Navigable water**- bodies of water (such as rivers, canals or lakes) where the water is deep enough, wide enough, and slow enough for a vessel to travel.
> ¤ **Fixed platform**- a platform that is mostly stationary. It is not considered a vessel and so the Jones Act will not apply to accidents that occur on fixed platforms.

his accident occurs on the platform, Louisiana law will apply to any possible claim that the employee may have against any third parties. The same is true for individuals who are injured on or near docks within state waters. Very often the law of the state where the dock was located will apply to such injuries.

Main Points:

1. General maritime law applies to any injury or claim that occurs on "navigable" water.
2. Navigable water is any body of water (rivers, lakes, canals, and oceans) that a vessel can travel on.
3. Injuries on fixed platforms are not covered under maritime law.

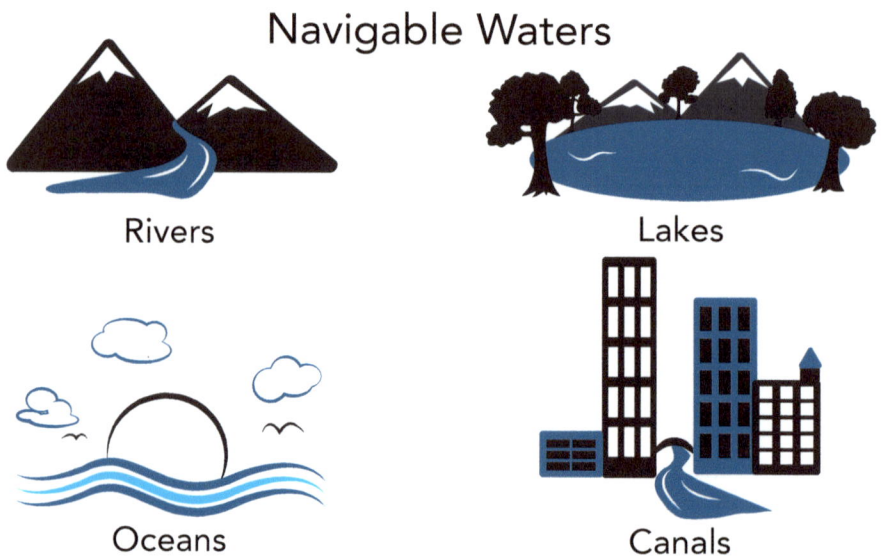

JONES ACT HIDDEN SECRETS

The Jones Act is a federal statute which provides extensive protections to an employee who is injured while working. It is one of few federal laws that truly protects employees who are involved in workplace accidents. If the Jones Act applies to your situation, you are actually considered a "ward" of the court. This term dates back more than a hundred years and essentially means that the court has a duty to protect you and your rights. Unfortunately, today this term does not carry as much weight as it used to many years ago. Nonetheless, injured seamen under the Jones Act are still technically considered wards of the court. This gives you an idea of the significant protections that the Jones Act gives to injured employees.

If you are injured on land while driving an automobile within your state, in all likelihood the law of your state will apply to your injury. In a similar way, you must satisfy certain "status" requirements before maritime law and/or the Jones Act will even apply to your situation. In general, you will qualify for protection under the Jones Act (and file a claim under the Jones Act) if you are a "seaman" who is more or less permanently assigned to a vessel in navigation. We will discuss this definition later (see page 14).

Why Is the Jones Act so Important to You?

The Jones Act allows an injured employee to collect money damages for any of the employer's negligence which may have caused or contributed to the employee's injury. If your company or coworker was at fault in causing or contributing to your accident and injury, you can collect compensation from your employer for your injury and damages. This law is very different than the general rule that an employee cannot sue his employer even if the employer caused his injury.

Determining your status is the first and foremost step in better understanding the situation surrounding your injury.

Main Points:
1. The Jones Act protects injured employees.
2. The Jones Act allows employees to collect damages from negligent employers.
3. The Jones Act only applies to seamen.

> ¤ **Jones Act**- a federal statute which provides extensive protections to an employee who is assigned to a vessel and is injured while working offshore.
> ¤ **Damages**- money that is awarded through a court process to an injured worker who has been hurt through the negligent or wrongful actions of someone else.
> ¤ **Negligence**- refers to the failure of someone else to take the necessary precautions to prevent injury to another.

ARE YOU A SEAMAN?

When Does the Jones Act Apply to You?

The first issue which must be addressed in any offshore injury concerns the "status" of the employee. Determining the status of an injured employee can be very difficult.

Although status in many cases is easy to determine (for example, with supply vessel employees or tug boat employees who are clearly seaman), the status of many cases are not determined until a hearing in court. Your status at the time of your accident can make a huge difference in the amount you may be allowed to receive for your injury.

In order to be covered under the Jones Act you must be considered a "seaman." This means that you are (1) more or less permanently (2) assigned to a vessel or fleet of vessels (3) in navigation. You must satisfy all three requirements in order to be considered a seaman and have the Jones Act apply to your claim. We will look more closely at what these requirements mean.

> ¤ **Seaman**- to be considered a seaman you must spend 30 percent or more of your time on a vessel that is navigation.

"More or Less Permanently"

The requirement that you be "more or less permanently" assigned to a vessel in navigation simply means that you spend *at least* 30 percent of your time aboard vessels while working for your employer. Many individuals will easily satisfy this requirement including traditional captains of vessels as well as oil rig workers who work aboard certain types of oil rigs in the Gulf of Mexico. Other individuals, however, will need to determine if their employer has assigned them to work aboard a vessel enough times during their period of employment. In some instances it is important to calculate the number of days that the employee was assigned to work aboard a vessel as opposed to assignments on land or on fixed platforms. Remember, the requirement is that at least 30 percent of your time be spent aboard "vessels" in order to qualify as a seaman under the Jones Act.

"Assigned to a Vessel"

Many will debate whether you are assigned to a "vessel." Some structures are clearly vessels: traditional supply boats, crew boats, tug boats and moving barges. Employees who are more or less permanently assigned to work aboard such structures easily satisfy the requirement that they be assigned to a vessel. In the Gulf of Mexico certain types of oil rigs have also been deter mined to be vessels. These include jack-up rigs, semi-submersible rigs and the more recent drill ships. Rig workers assigned to these types of structures will also satisfy the requirement of being assigned to a vessel.

"In Navigation"

Finally, you must be on a vessel that is mobile (able to move) or in navigation. The vessel need not be *moving* at the time of your injury. Rather the vessel must not be dry docked or out of service for good. Certain specialty structures may or may not be considered a vessel depending upon their mobility at the time of the employee's assignment or injury aboard the structure. These structures include work barges which may or may not have been rendered "work platforms." In the Gulf of Mexico fixed platforms as well as SPARs are *not* considered vessels. These structures are essentially permanently fixed to the ocean bed, so they are considered islands of the state off of which they sit. Injuries on fixed platforms and SPARs will not qualify for the Jones Act.

Main Points:

1. Three main factors define you as a seaman: you are (1) more or less permanently (2) assigned to a vessel or fleet of vessels (3) in navigation.

UNDERSTANDING YOUR OFFSHORE INJURY

2. You must spend at least 30 percent of your time aboard a vessel.

3. Traditional supply boats, crew boats, tug boats, moving barges, jack-up rigs, semi-submersible rigs and the more recent drill ships are clearly vessels.

4. SPARS, fixed platforms, and structures permanently fixed to the sea floor are not considered vessels.

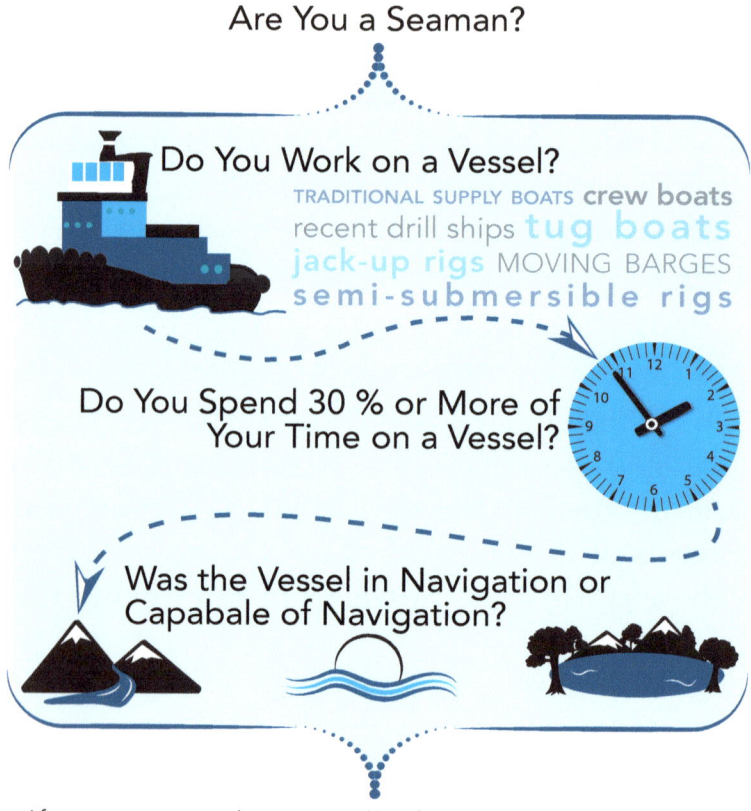

ARE YOU BEING KEPT SAFE?

The Jones Act provides comprehensive safety rules in the favor of the employee. Most individuals working offshore have no idea of the significant rights and safety rules that apply to their day-to-day activities. Unfortunately, many companies routinely violate these rules.

"Safe Place to Work" Safety Rule

Under the Jones Act an employee has a right to a "safe place to work." This is one of the broadest rules of the Jones Act and it applies to many situations which can cause injuries. If your case is decided by a judge or jury, that judge or jury will specifically determine if you were given a "safe place to work."

If you have suffered an injury and you think that the injury may have been caused because your workplace was unsafe, this could be a violation of the Jones Act.

What is Considered to be "Unsafe"?

Very often when we speak to potential clients we are told that "we always did the job that way" even though specific rules and regulations were being violated. Many times these individuals are not even aware that their safety was in jeopardy. To combat this, we have compiled a list of some of the most common unsafe conditions offshore:

- Inexperienced or inadequately trained crew
- Faulty machinery
- Poorly maintained conditions or work areas
- Defective equipment
- Existence of dangerous conditions (such as grease or oil on surfaces)
- Size of crew is insufficient (improper manpower)
- Equipment isn't fit for its intended use
- Recreation facilities are unsafe
- No appropriate safety equipment and gear
- Slick surfaces such as on the deck
- Old, rusted equipment

"Proper Training" Safety Rule

Under the Jones Act your employer also has duties to train you properly, to supervise your work activities properly, and to provide enough employees to do the jobs to which you are assigned.

Often newly hired employees will not be properly trained on how to do a job. Employers routinely refer to "on-the-job training" (OJT). We have found that this type of training can be insufficient for many of the detailed, complicated jobs which require experienced workers. Unfortunately, the more dangerous procedures tend to be harder to perform. Sometimes the newest employee will be given the hardest job because the more experienced, more senior employees do not want to perform the harder job, leaving the new, less experienced worker doing the most dangerous jobs.

"Proper Manpower" Safety Rule

Employers must also provide enough workers for the job to be performed safely under the Jones Act. Some employers will continually perform a job without sufficient employees simply because "it has always been done that way." The Jones Act addresses this exact situation and the judge or jury in your case will be told that simply performing a job repeatedly the same way does not necessarily make the procedure safe. This is particularly true concerning procedures which are performed infrequently. In these situations, many employers will not have sufficient manpower to perform the job because it is not a routine procedure. Nonetheless, these employers very often simply perform the job with the crew members that are available at that time.

"Industry Standards" Safety Rule

There are many industry-specific rules and regulations which also apply under the Jones Act. These industry standards include the American Petroleum Institute's (API) standards which apply to the operation of cranes offshore as well as rigging of cranes and slings. Under the API rules, the crane operator is always "in charge" of any procedure being performed by the crane. The crane operator is also required to have a flag man present on all lifts and the crane operator is ultimately responsible for the rigging of all loads.

"Coast Guard Regulations"

The United States Coast Guard rules also apply under the Jones Act since the employee is assigned to a Coast Guard "vessel." This is the reason that the Coast Guard will typically investigate serious injuries which occur under the Jones Act. Coast Guard regulations include keeping the vessel safe and making sure that there are no dangerous trip or slip hazards aboard the vessel. All walkways also have to be properly marked under Coast Guard regulations.

"OSHA Regulations"

Finally, OSHA regulations also provide guidance under the Jones Act. OSHA has detailed requirements that inspections be performed of workplaces. OSHA also requires that employees be given "safe" work places and that all equipment and machinery be working properly. Typically, OSHA will have detailed specific rules such as requiring that the front of steps be marked with some type of visible marker including yellow paint.

> ### Insider Tip
> You can find all of the OSHA maritime regulations here:
>
> http://www.osha.gov/pls/oshaweb/owasrch.search_form?p_doc_type=STANDARDS&p_toc_level=1&p_keyvalue=Maritime
>
> You can also type "OSHA regulations" into Google and click the first link. You will then need to click the third link labeled "Maritime" near the middle of the page.

Main Points:

1. As an offshore worker, there are many rules in place that are meant to protect your safety and your life. Unfortunately, employers do not always follow these regulations.
2. You are entitled to a "safe place to work" and it is

1. your employer's responsibility to provide this to you.

2. Some examples of "unsafe" conditions are inexperienced or improperly trained crew, faulty machinery, poor maintenance, defective equipment, dangerous conditions, insufficient crew, tools used improperly, unsafe recreation facilities, lack of proper safety equipment and gear, slick surfaces, and old, rusted equipment.

3. Your employer also has the duty to properly train you and your coworkers.

4. The Jones Act further requires that employers provide enough workers to perform the assigned job safely.

5. The Jones Act also specifies that employers must follow the additional guidelines provided by the American Petroleum Institute, the Coast Guard, and OSHA.

Insider Insight
5 Tactics Your Company Will Use After Your Injury

1. <u>Most maritime companies try to take a recorded statement from you immediately following your injury.</u> Many companies will hire insurance company representatives to "investigate" your claim. These representatives typically tell you that they are trying to help you with your claim and they "just want to document your injury."

Do not believe these insurance company representatives. They work for your company, NOT you. In almost all cases the reason they are taking a recorded statement from you is to ask detailed questions about your background, accident and injury in order to (1) prove that they were not at fault for your accident, (2) prove you may have been at fault for your accident, and (3) catch you in a misstatement about anything (see item 5 below). You should never provide a tape recorded statement to your company or its insurance representative.

2. <u>Your company will obtain surveillance on you.</u> Maritime companies try to obtain surveillance not only after a lawsuit is filed but, incredibly, sometimes within days of your accident and injury. We have seen many cases in which within two to three days the company

has hired private investigators to document the injured worker's daily activities. If you are continuing to work outside and trying to perform regular activities following your injury, your company may be trying to obtain videotape of such activities. Very often companies will refuse to pay for medical treatment based upon videotape that they have obtained of you.

3. <u>Your company will insist that you receive treatment from their chosen doctor.</u> Even though maritime law is very clear that an injured worker has the right to choose his own treating physician, almost every maritime company will *insist* that an injured worker receive medical treatment from a doctor that it chooses. This can be devastating to you and your future.

If you receive treatment from a company-chosen physician, sometimes it is impossible to prove the nature of your injury. Most company-chosen physicians refuse or delay required medical testing which could prove the nature of your injury. Most company physicians will simply suggest that you wait several weeks following your injury to see if it resolves itself. These doctors very often encourage you to "try" to return to

...... Insider Insight ......

work as soon as possible regardless of whether you have had basic medical testing performed. And once you return to work, it is very difficult to get approval for additional medical treatment since the company will claim that you were "able to return to work."

4. <u>Your company will refuse to let you choose your own treating physician.</u> This tactic goes hand-in-hand with tactic 3 above when your company insists that you receive treatment from a doctor that it has chosen. Very often your company will tell you that you must see a company-chosen doctor at the start of your treatment.

Unfortunately, once this doctor declares that you are released to "full duty" work, your company will then use this as an excuse to refuse you the right to see your own chosen physician. Once you begin treatment from a company-chosen physician, very often it is impossible for you to receive treatment from other doctors later on. It is always best to insist that you be seen by a doctor that you trust and that you choose. You have the right to select your own treating doctor.

5. <u>Your company will make every effort possible to</u>

Insider Insight

catch you in a misstatement. This is one of the most frustrating tactics used by offshore maritime companies in fighting maritime injury claims. Every single case we have handled involved company lawyers trying to catch the injured party in a misstatement (or as they say, a "lie").

The nature of the misstatement does not make any difference. For example, if you told the company during your recorded statement that you had never sustained any injuries in the past, yet years ago you temporarily suffered a 3 month knee injury from which you fully recovered, this misstatement could end up ruining your case even if it has nothing to do with your offshore injury.

You will be put on trial during your case and any misstatement that you make, regardless of how inconsequential, may ruin your case. It is very important that you understand your company will be prosecuting you from the beginning of your case during your offshore maritime claim and everything you say and do will be questioned by the company as well as the company lawyer.

They want to focus your case away from your injury and on other issues, including any trivial incorrect statements you may have made in the past.

COMMON MYTHS DEBUNKED

There are several common issues that appear in many Jones Act cases. We have found that many of our clients have specific questions concerning the following issues.

They Can't Make You Sign: Accident Reports

There is absolutely no requirement that an employee complete a written accident report under the Jones Act. Although it is certainly best to document your accident and injury with a written accident report, the Jones Act does not prohibit your claim from being filed if an accident report was not completed. Very often an employee will report his accident and injury to a supervisor who tells the employee to delay completing a report in order to determine if the injury is serious. Then, when the employee attempts to complete the written report later, he is told that he can no longer complete the report at that time. Just remember, completing an accident report is absolutely not required to file suit and successfully collect damages under the Jones Act.

The Jones Act requires only that you prove that you suffered an injury at work for which your employer was responsible. You may prove such without a written report. We have successfully proved accidents by using employees' medical records, the testimony of their coworkers, or their own testimony.

Recorded Statements

An employee is not required to give a recorded statement under the Jones Act. Many companies will immediately take a tape-recorded statement from an injured employee following his accident. Providing a tape-recorded statement does not in any way help or strengthen your case. In fact, most tape-recorded statements will hurt a worker's Jones Act claim.

Typically employees are told that they need to provide recorded statements in order to receive medical treatment and to properly document their accidents. Again, there is absolutely no requirement under the Jones Act or any other law that the employee provides a recorded statement. Nonetheless, many workers will provide statements believing that it is necessary in order for them to receive medical treatment.

When the statement is taken, detailed questions concerning the accident are asked, including whether there was anything unsafe that caused or contributed to the accident. Many employees have not had time to think through the accident and typically will answer very quickly that the company was not at fault for the accident (and they just want to get medical treatment and get back to work). Often employees believe that their injuries may be insignificant and believe that they will keep their job with the employer. Sometimes employees are taking medication when they provide the recorded statement and they simply do not understand or listen carefully to the questions.

In general, it is best to *refuse* to give a recorded statement following your accident. You may simply inform the company very politely that you either have completed a written report or will complete a written report concerning the accident at which time you can carefully provide answers to any necessary questions. If your company insists that you provide a recorded statement, your company is protecting itself, not you.

Your Injury, Your Doctor of Choice

Under the Jones Act you are allowed to choose your own treating physician following your injury. This is perhaps the rule most violated by companies. It makes perfect sense that your employer would not want you to select a good, *unbiased* physician for your injury. Your employer seldom has any desire for you to receive immediate proper medical treatment which could potentially prove the seriousness of your injury. Instead, most employers will provide you with a "company doctor" who will delay running necessary tests or delay providing specialized treatment for your injury. Not only can this be detrimental to your overall health but also to any future claim you may want to have. This tactic typically serves two purposes.

First, the company can later say that your injury was not very serious since you received only basic, conservative treatment for several months following your injury. You will also not have proper testing performed to show the nature and extent of your injury during the first few months of your recovery.

Second, if a company doctor treats you for several weeks or even months and then declares that you have reached maximum improvement and you do not need any further treatment, your company will typically refuse to provide you with any further medical treatment on these grounds.

So, while you may think you are cooperating with the company by going to see a doctor that they have selected to treat you, in reality you may be making it very hard for yourself to receive proper medical treatment if the company-selected doctor discharges you. It is always best to insist that you receive treatment from a doctor that you select and trust. It is also best to insist that all proper medical testing be performed as soon as possible following your injury.

Their Doctor, Their Mistake

If you receive negligent medical treatment from a doctor selected by your company to treat you, your company is responsible for this negligent treatment. Typically this occurs when a company-selected doctor delays treatment of a condition that could have been properly treated early on. It may also occur nowadays especially when individuals receive treatment in foreign countries while working overseas. We have handled several cases in which the employee did not receive proper treatment from an overseas medical clinic selected by their employer. In these circumstances the employer is responsible for the negligent medical treatment as well as any damage caused by the treatment.

Main Points:

1. You're not required by law to complete a written accident report, especially not immediately after your injury when you're dazed. You should do one when you are clear headed and are able to reflect on the incident.
2. Despite what your company may say, you <u>do not</u> have to provide a recorded statement.

1. You can and should choose your own doctor. You are not required to use the company doctor for your injury. If you receive treatment from the company doctor, it may be hard to receive future medical treatment.
2. Your company is responsible for any negligent medical treatment you receive from their chosen doctor or hospital.

3 Maritime Injury Myths Debunked

Myth 1:
You must give an accident report.
Fact 1:
Accident reports are not required.

Myth 2:
You must give a recorded statement.
Fact 2:
Statements are not required by law.

Myth 3:
You must see the company doctor.
Fact 3:
You can choose your own doctor.

ENOUGH'S ENOUGH

LET THE LAW FIGHT FOR YOU

Who is at Fault?

There are two important points to remember when you consider filing a suit against your employer under the Jones Act. First, in order to receive compensation under the Jones Act you must prove that your company or your coworkers were negligent. The Jones Act is a fault-based statute, meaning that you only collect damages if your company was at fault. This fault can take many forms, including the improper or unsafe acts of your coworkers, an unsafe workplace, or unsafe or improper instructions. It is often easy to show that your injury could have been avoided if your company acted in a safer manner.

Second, the Jones Act allows your employer to allege and argue "comparative fault" on your part. This means that if your company can prove that you caused

> ¤ **Comparative fault**- (also known as comparative responsibility) a legal policy that compares the fault of each party (both defendants and prosecution) for a single injury. This is determined by looking at how responsible each party is for causing the accident.

UNDERSTANDING YOUR OFFSHORE INJURY

or contributed to your own accident and injury, this amount of fault will reduce your recovery by that percentage. For example, if your company proves through evidence and testimony that you contributed 50 percent to your own accident, any damages which you are entitled to under the Jones Act will be reduced by 50 percent.

> **Insider Insight**
> The Jones Act's comparative fault statute is one of the main reasons why a company will immediately blame an injured worker for his/her own accident. This statute allows companies to argue that you were partly to blame for your accident and if they convince the judge or jury, they could potentially reduce what they have to pay you for your injury.

It is critical that an injured employee understand the nature of the Jones Act in this regard. This comparative fault rule fully explains why almost all companies will immediately blame an injured

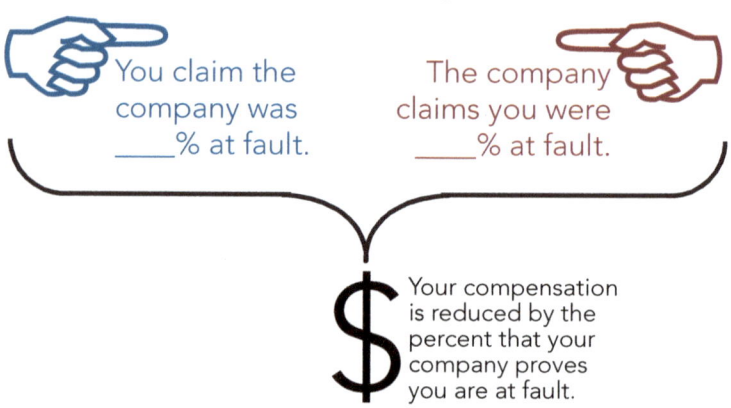

The Jones Act's Comparative Fault

You claim the company was ____% at fault.

The company claims you were ____% at fault.

Your compensation is reduced by the percent that your company proves you are at fault.

46 www.JonesActLaw.com

employee for their own accident. <u>It also explains why a company will immediately take a recorded statement from the injured employee and discuss the way that the accident happened during the statement.</u> In short, the company is simply trying to defend itself early and quickly against any type of claim that you may later file under the Jones Act. Our office strongly encourages injured workers to state clearly why their accident happened, including listing any fault on the part of the company or their coworkers on the accident reports. Injured employees should also be sure to list any dangerous condition or unsafe equipment which may have caused or contributed to their accident.

> **Insider Tip**
> When submitting an accident report, always state clearly how your accident happened and if anyone contributed to it. You should also list any dangerous or unsafe conditions or equipment that may have caused your injury.

The Jones Act's Burden of Proof

Under the Jones Act an employee has a "featherweight" burden of proof in regard to causation of his injuries. This is a very important and favorable rule under the Jones Act. When you present your maritime case to a judge or jury, you must be able to prove that your injury was caused by your accident. The Jones Act greatly helps you by requiring only a "featherweight" burden of proof to show that your injury was caused by the accident. This rule is especially helpful if you have previously injured the same part of your body as you injured in your current accident. By using the featherweight burden of proof, you may be able to successfully show that your current injury was caused by the most recent accident, even if you had previously injured the same part of your body many years ago.

Main Points:

1. To receive compensation under the Jones Act, you must prove that your company or coworkers did something wrong to cause your injury.

2. Your employer is allowed to counterargue that you caused your own injury. This is called "comparative fault" and allows them to reduce how much they pay you by the percentage you caused your own injury.

3. Your employer will almost always try to prove that you caused your own injury. They will do this by keeping you under surveillance, by getting you to sign accident reports that claim you were at fault, by using their own doctor, and by getting recorded statements from you.

4. The Jones Act has a featherweight burden of proof, which means it takes less for you to prove that your injury was caused by your accident.

TYPES OF COMPENSATION UNDER JONES ACT LAW

What Can You Get from a Jones Act Claim?

Under the Jones Act you are entitled to collect any damages which are directly related to your accident. Typically these damages will include pain and suffering, medical expenses and loss of wages and fringe benefits.

Pain & Suffering

There are two types of pain and suffering damages that you can collect under the Jones Act: past pain and suffering and future pain and suffering. The damages allowed for pain and suffering depend greatly upon the nature of your injury. You will be allowed to collect damages for both past as well as future pain and suffering if you prove these damages at trial.

In regards to past pain and suffering damages, your testimony as well as the testimony of your treating doctors will be very important. We also routinely call as witnesses an injured employee's spouse or friends to

> ¤ **Pain and suffering**- physical or emotional stress caused by your injury.

testify as to how the injury has affected the employee's life.

However, with future pain and suffering damages it is often best to rely upon your treating physicians who can testify as to whether or not your condition will improve or worsen in the future. Judges and juries are allowed to estimate the amount and type of pain and suffering that you will most likely experience in the future, and under the Jones Act they are allowed to award money damages for this suffering even though it has not occurred.

Medical Expenses

Like pain and suffering, you can get compensation for past and future medical expenses related to your injury.

Loss of Wages

You are also entitled to recover for past and future loss of wages and fringe benefits that are directly related to your injury. Our office routinely works with experienced economists who will calculate the exact value of

> ¤ **Loss wages**- the income you would have earned if you were not injured.

your past and future loss of wages and fringe benefits. In almost all cases, an expert economist is required to predict future loss of wages. Most courts will not allow an employee to collect loss of future wages and future fringe benefits unless an expert economist has made these calculations for the jury.

Calculating your loss of past and future wages greatly depends upon the amount of money that you were earning at the time of your injury. However, the Jones Act also allows you to be awarded money based upon promotions and raises in pay which, in all likelihood, you would have received had you kept working. This can be very important for long-term employees who have a proven history of receiving pay raises over their years of employment.

Our office is very careful to calculate future wages assuming that certain employees may have received pay raises in the future. This can make the difference between collecting the amount to which you are truly entitled rather than simply the amount which appears on your current paycheck.

Loss of Fringe Benefits

One of the great benefits of working offshore or on a vessel is the significant fringe benefits that many mar

itime employees receive. Most often you will no longer receive these fringe benefits after you are injured. Fringe benefits typically include:
- Meals provided to the employee while working
- Retirement benefits
- Health insurance
- Disability insurance

Our office will obtain all of your pay records including the value of your fringe benefits and use this information to calculate the true value of your past and future economic losses, including loss of fringe benefits. Sometimes your loss of fringe benefits can amount to almost as much as your loss of actual wages.

Main Points:

1. There are four main types of damages you can collect under the Jones Act: pain and suffering, medical expenses, loss wages, and loss of fringe benefits.
2. To collect past pain and suffering, often you will need the testimony of your doctor and another individual who has seen how your injury affects you. For future pain and suffering you will mostly rely on your physician's testimony.
3. To collect loss of wages or fringe benefits, you will need an expert economist to prove how much you would have earned over the years.

MAKING THE LEAP

How Soon Should You Hire a Lawyer?

Claims filed under the Jones Act must be filed within <u>three years</u> of the employee's injury. Please note that it is critical to file your claim as soon as possible after your injury if you have sustained a serious injury. Individuals who choose to wait until the end of the three year period may find that documents have been lost or destroyed or witnesses simply do not remember important details concerning the employee's accident. Although claims under the Jones Act do not need to be filed until three years from the date of the injury, usually it is important to file the suit much sooner.

Where Should You File Your Claim?

A suit filed under the Jones Act can be filed in either state court or federal court. There is a legal principle known as the "savings to suitors" clause that provides that even though the Jones Act is a federal statute, claims under the Jones Act may still be filed in state courts, which recognize federal claims under the Jones Act. However, if you file your claim in federal court under the Jones Act, you alone have the right to select either a judge or jury trial. By contrast, typically if a Jones Act claim is filed in state court, either party will have the right to a trial by jury. Depending upon the facts of your case and the federal judge to whom your case may be assigned, sometimes it is better to select a trial by judge rather than a trial by jury.

The location of the courthouse where you are allowed to file suit varies from case to case. Normally you will be allowed to choose between several locations to file suit. If you file suit in federal court, any federal court in the United States has the ability to hear your case.

However, in federal court there is a rule known as "forum non conveniens" which essentially requires that the federal court you select be located near some of the relevant activities that did, or will, occur in your case. This can include the location of the original accident or the location of your treating doctors or the location of key witnesses in your case including yourself. If you file suit in state court, there is usually also a requirement that some of the activities

> ¤ **Forum non conveniens**- a legal rule that allows courts to require a case be tried in the jurisdiction that is most appropriate to the parties involved. This means that the federal court must be near some of the relevant activities that did or will occur.

in your case have occurred near that location. This requirement can often be satisfied if the company has an office located nearby or if you were sent offshore from that location.

Our office regularly files suits in federal and state court in south Louisiana on behalf of workers from Florida, Alabama, Mississippi and other southern states, since their employers have offices in Louisiana and/or the employee worked out of south Louisiana.

Finding the Right Person for the Job

It can be difficult deciding to hire a maritime lawyer much less researching them. There are dozens and dozens of "maritime" law firms listed online but which ones should you choose?

Often people base their decisions on factors that would apply to other areas of their life but do not necessarily apply to finding the right maritime attorney. Some might use location, the size of a billboard message, or a catchy song to help them decide who to choose.

However, we believe that the most important factor you want to consider is whether or not the attorney is focused on your circumstances. If you are putting your future in someone's hands, it should be in the hands of an experienced and focused maritime attorney who knows your problems, knows how to solve your problems, and has the resources to do it.

> **Insider Tip**
>
> Visit the below link to learn how to effectively research attorneys online and find the right maritime attorney for you.
>
> http://www.jonesactlaw.com/library/researching-maritime-law-firms.cfm

Main Points:

1. If you're going to file a claim, you must do it no later than three years after your injury. We recommend you do it sooner than that as the important documents related to your injury (such as your accident report, medical tests, statements, etc.) may have conveniently "disappeared" by that time.
2. The Jones Act allows you to file a claim in a federal or state court. We often choose federal court as it allows you to choose whether your case is heard by a judge or a jury.
3. If you're going to hire an attorney to handle your case, you should hire a maritime attorney that focuses on your problem.

......................................Insider Insight......
5 Qualities Your Jones Act Maritime Lawyer "Must Have"

1. <u>Must Focus On Jones Act And Maritime Injury Cases.</u> When you need to see a doctor, you want to go see a doctor who specializes in the type of injury that you have suffered. In the same way, you should hire a maritime lawyer who focuses the practice on handling Jones Act and maritime injury claims.

If you need to have open heart surgery, you would want to have a heart surgeon who specializes in that type of surgery. If you need to have knee surgery, you would want to see a doctor who specializes in knee surgeries. Likewise, when you have a serious maritime injury, you should find a good maritime lawyer who focuses the practice on handling maritime injury cases. Many "general practice" lawyers in your area are very nice and know a little bit about lots of different laws. Unfortunately, these lawyers typically are not experienced enough with complicated Jones Act and maritime laws to truly handle a maritime injury claim.

2. <u>Must Have Extensive Courtroom Experience.</u> It is amazing how many attorneys never actually go to court to argue aspects of the case or try cases before judges and juries. Maritime lawsuits are defended by the insurance companies and company lawyers. These

company lawyers will fight every issue in your maritime case and this often involves arguing motions before the court. Very often Jones Act and maritime cases are prepared all the way up until the point of trial, at which time a fair settlement can finally be reached. If not, your case will need to be presented to a jury. Your maritime injury attorney will most likely spend as much time in court on your case as he will working on the case outside of court. It is very important that your attorney have extensive courtroom experience so that he can successfully handle your case.

3.   <u>Must Have Significant Financial Resources (Money!)</u>. Your maritime injury claim will be expensive to present successfully to a judge or jury. Typically, your claim will involve loss of past and future wages and fringe benefits. An economic expert is necessary to testify regarding this issue at trial. Your case may require a liability expert to show what the company did wrong that caused your injury. These experts require payment up front and your maritime attorney will be responsible for hiring and funding these experts until your case can settle. For every dollar that the company spends in an effort to defend your claim, your attorney must be prepared to finance your case in a similar way.

> ¤ **Motion**- a legal request for the judge to determine some aspect of the case.

······························Insider Insight······

4. <u>Must Have a Great Team.</u> Your maritime injury claim will require office resources and skills as well as financial resources. In order to successfully prove your case, hours and hours of effort and work will be spent in accumulating the necessary documents and obtaining the necessary testimony to prove your case at trial.

This work includes getting all of your medical and work records, arranging and paying for medical treatment so that you can prove your injury, hiring and working with experts in regards to your damages, working with experts to prove the fault of the company, scheduling and taking depositions from key witnesses, and organizing all of these documents and information so that they can be successfully presented at court. Your maritime attorney needs to have an office staff that is experienced and able to prepare your case.

5. <u>Must Be Ready To Prepare Your Case Fully.</u> This may be one of the most important requirements of your maritime injury attorney. Very often successful attorneys will have significant financial resources, office staff and even have experience handling maritime claims. However, many of these attorneys will accept lots of cases but truly pursue only a few of these cases.

> ¤ **Deposition**- a legal question and answer session that is recorded and later used in court as testimony.

Insider Insight

In other words, they may accept your claim and if they eventually determine that they do not view your case as a "high dollar case," they may limit their work on your case. Your attorney must be ready to prepare your case fully for trial. When you hire your attorney, you should ask if he is truly ready and able to prepare your case fully in order to obtain a good settlement or trial result.

FILING SUIT UNDER GENERAL MARITIME LAW

Lawsuits filed under general maritime law must be filed within three years of the accident that gives rise to the suit. It is usually best to file the claim as soon as possible to prevent the loss of valuable records.

These suits can be filed either in state court or federal court. There is no right to a trial by jury under a claim based solely on general maritime law.

However, when a general maritime law claim is combined with another basis for jurisdiction within the court, including the Jones Act and/or diversity of the parties, the injured party will have the right to a trial by jury.

While only "seamen" can file suit under the Jones Act, any individual can file a suit under general maritime law if he or she has been involved in an accident that occurred on navigable waters.

Typically passengers aboard cruise line vessels as well as offshore workers who are injured by non-employer third parties will file their claims under general maritime law.

Negligence under General Maritime Law

Maritime law provides that a party is responsible for any damages caused by their "negligence." Negligence under general maritime law is defined as failing to do what a reasonable person would have done under similar circumstances. This is the "reasonable person" test which also applies to most state-based negligence claims.

Typically, a party can prove negligence under maritime law by showing that the defendant failed to take some type of action which should have been taken or by showing that the defendant acted in an improper or unsafe manner. In order to recover under a general maritime law claim, you must prove that the defendant was "negligent."

General maritime law also provides for comparative fault against the party filing suit. This means that the defendant can and will try to claim that the injured party was responsible in whole or in part for causing his or her own injury.

Injured offshore workers who file suits against non-employer third parties will still need to show that they did not in any way cause or contribute to their own accident. If the injured party is found to be at fault for his or her own accident, then the damages are reduced by the percentage of fault. So, if the judge or jury finds that the injured party was 20 percent at fault in causing his or her own accident, the damages will be reduced by 20 percent.

Finally, maritime law will also allow defendants to reduce the amount of damages they must pay by any other non party's fault.

For example, if another company caused your accident and that company is not named in your lawsuit, then the defendant in your lawsuit may try to place blame upon the unnamed company.

If the defendant is successful, your damages will be reduced by the amount of fault placed upon the unnamed company. This is why when you file suit, it is very important to name as a defendant any party that may be responsible for your accident.

> ¤ **Seaworthy**- a vessel is seaworthy if it is reasonably fit for its intended purpose and if all equipment or accessories are also fit for the intended purposes.

General Maritime Law Unseaworthiness

One of the main principles of general maritime law is the doctrine of seaworthiness. Under general maritime law a vessel owner must provide a "seaworthy" vessel. The law states that every vessel must be "reasonably fit for its intended purpose." This includes not only the vessel itself but also its equipment and "appurtenances," or accessories.

If a piece of equipment breaks or malfunctions, and this contributes to your accident, typically a claim will be filed under general maritime law under the doctrine of seaworthiness (along with any other appropriate claim such as a Jones Act claim). The doctrine of seaworthiness only applies to the vessel owner.

Damages under General Maritime Law

General maritime law provides that injured parties shall be compensated for all damages related to their injuries. This includes
- Past and future loss of wages
- Loss of fringe benefits
- Past and future physical/mental pain and suffering

> ¤ **Punitive damages**- these damages go above and beyond typical damages and are aimed at "punishing" the defendant. Punitive damages are not typically awarded, but you should still seek these damages.

- Past and future medical expenses

Please note that if you have filed a Jones Act claim along with a general maritime law claim, you cannot collect double the damages.

Punitive Damages Under General Maritime Law

General maritime law allows a party to seek punitive damages against the defendant. While the law is very complicated as to whether all injured maritime workers can seek punitive damages under maritime law, we typically ask for such in almost all cases we file.

Maintenance and Cure under General Maritime Law

Under general maritime law an employer has an obligation to provide its injured employee with "maintenance and cure." Typically maintenance and cure claims

> ¤ **Maintenance**-defined by the law as the amount it costs for you to maintain yourself on land as your employer did at sea. You are entitled to receive maintenance if you are injured.
> ¤ **Cure**-defined as medical expenses that are reasonable and related to your injury. You are allowed to select your own choice of treating physician and your company must pay for any medical treatment that is reasonable and related to your injury.

UNDERSTANDING YOUR OFFSHORE INJURY

> **Insider Tip**
>
> You will receive in the mail a free Maintenance & Cure checklist as well as a Monthly Expense Letter to fill out and give to your company. If you do not receive these resources, please call us at 504-680-4100 and we will send them immediately.

are filed by injured seamen since these individuals are necessarily filing suit against their employers.

The law states that all ambiguities or doubts in regard to a maintenance and cure claim should be resolved in favor of the seaman. This doctrine gives you an idea of how strong your rights are to maintenance and cure benefits. Maintenance is defined by the law as the amount it costs for you to maintain yourself on land as your employer did at sea.

In other words maintenance typically includes the costs for your lodging, food and monthly bills while you are injured. Most companies pay a fixed rate of $15.00 to $30.00 per day as maintenance. <u>There is absolutely no basis in the law for the payment of this amount.</u>

Most companies arbitrarily select this amount and argue that this amount has been paid for many years to injured seamen. It is *very* important that you seek the maintenance rate that is proper to pay your expenses while you are injured.

Cure is defined as medical expenses that are reasonable and related to your injury. You are allowed to select your own choice of treating physician and your company must pay for any medical treatment that is reasonable and related to your injury. If your employer fails to pay maintenance and cure, you can present a claim to the judge or jury that your employer was (1) unreasonable in failing to pay maintenance and cure and (2) arbitrary in refusing to pay maintenance and cure. There is an escalating standard as to whether your employer was, first, unreasonable, then, arbitrary.

If your employer is found to be unreasonable in failing to pay maintenance and cure, you may be awarded attorney fees associated with having to file suit in order to receive maintenance and cure.

Additionally, if your employer is found not only to be unreasonable but also arbitrary in failing to pay maintenance and cure, you may be awarded both punitive damages and damages for any worsening of your condition due to your employer's failure to pay your maintenance and cure.

Main Points:

1. Claims under general maritime law must be filed within three years of your injury.

1. Only seamen can file under the Jones Act, but any individual injured on navigable waters can file a general maritime claim.
2. Like the Jones Act, general maritime law allows for comparative fault.
3. The amount you receive for your claim could be reduced by the percentage of fault attributed to a third party.
4. Under maritime law, a vessel owner must provide a seaworthy vessel.
5. You cannot collect damages with both a Jones Act claim and a general maritime claim.
6. General maritime law allows for punitive damages.
7. An employer is obligated to pay for you to be able to maintain yourself on land as your employer did at sea. This is called maintenance.
8. Maintenance is the amount it costs for you to maintain yourself on land. This includes expenses such as rent, clothing, transportation, food, and other monthly expenses.
9. Your employer must pay for medical expenses that are reasonable and related to your injury. This is called cure.
10. Cure is considered the medical expenses that are reasonable and related to your injury.

MEDICAL INFO

COMMON MEDICAL TESTS FOR MARITIME AND OFFSHORE INJURIES

Arthroscopic Surgery

Although arthroscopic surgery is considered a "surgical" procedure, very often it is used to diagnose injuries which may not be visible with other non-invasive testing. Typically orthopedics will perform arthroscopic surgery on an individual's knee and shoulder areas. The purpose of this surgery is to not only repair any damage which may be seen but to also actually identify and visualize damage which may not have appeared on prior MRI and CT testing.

CT Scan

A CT scan (or CAT scan) is a form of enhanced X-ray that can diagnose soft tissue, organ and blood vessel type injuries. Very often a CT scan will be performed after an MRI scan to further diagnose or investigate the individual's injury. Typically the most helpful CT scans are performed "with contrast." This means that the individual will drink (or have IV injected) a type of dye before the CT scan is performed. The dye allows the CT scan to give a much more accurate, detailed image of the injured area.

Discogram/Myelogram

A discogram is a procedure during which dye is injected into a person's cervical or lumbar discs. The purpose of the test is to determine if the injected dye leaks out or goes beyond the subject disc.

Discograms can be a very accurate way to determine the full extent of a person's injury. Normally, healthy lumbar and cervical discs will hold the small amount of dye that is injected. This is because a normal, healthy disc is fully enclosed and encapsulated. If a lumbar or cervical disc has been injured, very often this will result in a tear to the disc. When the small amount of dye is injected into the disc, it will immediately leak out thus indicating that the disc has a hole or tear in it. A discogram is often followed by a CT scan which will take images of the disc and the dye in order to visualize if the dye has moved outside of the disc.

A myelogram is very similar to a discogram in that dye typically is injected around the injured lumbar or cervical area. A CT scan is then performed to view the area and the dye provides an enhanced image of any damage to that area.

EMG/Nerve Conduction Study

An electromyogram (EMG) is a test that is used to record the electrical activity of muscles. When muscles are active, they produce an electrical current. Typically an EMG is given at the same time as a nerve conduction study. The most common type of nerve conduction study is known as a Nerve Conduction Velocity (NCV) test.

These tests are used to diagnose nerve injuries and muscle damage. Very often they will be given to individuals who have suffered lower back injuries or neck injuries to diagnose nerve damage which may be occurring into the person's upper or lower extremities (arms or legs). The NCV will measure how quickly and completely a person's arm or leg nerve transfer 'information', or how quickly and completely they respond. If nerve damage has occurred, very often the response will be delayed or incomplete.

It is very important to note that most EMG/NCV tests are not 100 percent accurate. Most physicians will admit that the tests have at least a 10 percent margin of error. Very often individuals with nerve damage will have normal EMG/NCV tests even though they are experiencing nerve damage.

Epidural Steroid Injections

Also known as "epidural injections" or "steroid injections", this treatment is a series of injections typically given in a person's neck or lower back in an attempt to relieve pain from a damaged cervical or lumbar disc. Epidural injections can also be given in an individual's shoulder area as well as other parts of the body. Epidural injections are very often described as both therapeutic as well as diagnostic. This means that the injection is given to provide relief to the patient as well as potentially diagnose their injury. Most doctors believe that if the patient receives temporary relief for a period of days or even a few weeks from the injection, this means that the injection was most likely given at the source of the injury. In this way, the injection serves as a diagnostic tool to help the doctor identify the area of injury.

IDET

IDET stands for intradiscal electrothermic therapy. This procedure is minimally invasive and involves using a heated wire to seal any ruptures in the disc wall and to burn nerve endings to reduce the amount of pain. It aims to repair bulging discs before herniation.

MRI

A magnetic resonance imaging scan (MRI) is one of

the most common tests performed to diagnose most injuries to a neck, back, shoulder or knee. An MRI scan shows soft tissue and ligament damage and it provides a much greater detailed view than does a CT scan. MRIs will diagnose damaged lumbar and cervical discs as well as torn ligaments. If you have suffered any type of injury that has bothered you for more than a few days, most likely it is best to get an MRI scan performed. Many doctors will delay performing an MRI since they may not want to charge your company for the expense. It is important that you insist that all medical testing be performed, including MRIs. With today's technology an MRI should be considered a basic medical test.

The more traditional MRI is performed in a long tube. There is also a more advanced type of MRI known as a "stand up" MRI scan. A stand up MRI scan is taken while the individual is in a standing position (hence the name). Very often this can produce a more accurate MRI scan which more accurately reflects any type of herniated or damaged lumbar or cervical discs. This is because the scan is taken while the individual is actually placing weight on their lower back and neck.

Sympathetic Block

This type of test is performed as both treatment and a diagnostic. A sympathetic block is given to a pa tient to diagnose nerve damage typically into their lower legs, feet or ankles. The basic purpose of the sympathetic block is to "block" the nerve communication from the suspected injury to the person's brain. If the sympathetic block is successful, the person will receive relief since the injured part of the body temporarily will not communicate with the individual's brain. This result indicates to the doctor that the person is suffering from nerve damage at the point of the injury. If the sympathetic block is successful (and very often a series of them are performed), the doctor may consider permanently "disconnecting" that nerve such that it will no longer send messages of pain to the person's brain.

X-ray

An X-ray is a basic imaging scan of an individual's bones. An X-ray does not show soft tissue or ligament/tendon damage nor will it indicate nerve damage. Most doctors and health facilities will immediately perform an X-ray following an injury.

It is very important to understand that X-rays will not diagnose the majority of serious injuries including ligament/tendon damage, nerve damage, lumbar disc injuries or joint damage. These types of injuries need to be diagnosed with other tests including MRIs, CT scans, and nerve conduction studies.

INDEX

A
Advances 62
American Petroleum Institute 21

B
Blacklist 61

C
Coast Guard 21
Comparative fault 22, 25, 27, 34, 35, 36, 45, 47, 49, 55
Comparative responsibility.
    See Comparative fault
Cure 54

D
Damages 13
Deposition 48

F
Fixed platform 10
Forum non conveniens 43
Fringe benefits 40

G
General maritime law 10

J
Jones Act 13

L
Loss of wages 43

M
Maintenance 54, 63
Manpower 20
Maritime law
    See General maritime law

N
Navigable water 10
Negligence 13

O
On-the-job training 20
OSHA 22

P
Pain and suffering 38, 43
Punitive damages 53, 54, 63

S
Safe place to work 18
Safety 18
Seaman 14, 22, 25, 27, 34, 35, 36, 45, 47, 49, 55
Seaworthy 52
Soft tissue 63
Status 12

T
Training 19

EPILOGUE

It had been four weeks since Louis' accident. They had met with a very nice, local lawyer in their town a few days after Louis got home. The lawyer seemed nice enough, and he had helped their neighbor with a family matter years earlier. But he just didn't seem to know anything about maritime law or the Jones Act.

They had looked through the phone book but all of the ads were about 'car accidents' or 'medical malpractice.' The few that did mention maritime claims seemed to include them in a list with seven or eight other types of law. How could one lawyer be good at divorce cases, criminal cases and maritime claims?

Then Lisa saw an ad for a free book on maritime law and the Jones Act. She ordered it and the book arrived the next day. As they flipped through the pages, the book answered all of their questions.

Should Louis give a statement to the insurance company? Did he <u>have</u> to give a statement? Could he receive more medical treatment since he was still hurting? What rights did he have? The book gave them the answer to all these questions, *and more.*

They felt so relieved to finally know something about his future! Armed with answers to the most basic questions regarding his injury and his rights, they could now sit down and decide what to do. And they could make an <u>educated</u> decision about what direction to take their lives.

This felt good. Things were looking up...

WHY WE PRACTICE MARITIME LAW

My name is Timothy Young and for more than 20 years it has been my privilege to help injured offshore and maritime workers.

Something deep inside of me is stirred whenever I know that a company is trying to take advantage of an honest, hard-working employee who has had a serious injury through no fault of his own.

Most often there is an employer/employee relationship, and to me that makes it all the worse when an employer is twisting the laws or facts to get out of paying what it should for the serious damages it caused to one of its own employees.

Most offshore and maritime workers would prefer not to file a suit. They would rather go on with their careers and turn back the clock to before the accident happened. I understand that. But hoping to change the past won't make the future any better.

What we do is not simply gather evidence and experts to prove our client's claim in court. That's just the 'legal' part of it.

We also counsel our clients on their options and how to map out the best future they can have with the cards they were dealt. I can't think of a more important service we offer.

I often tell juries in closing arguments that they have a rare opportunity to help a fellow citizen and directly impact a person's life for the better. I tell them they should not waste that chance. I also feel we have that same opportunity with each new client we team up with.

I hope you found this book both helpful and encouraging during your current difficulties. Please phone us if you need anything or have any concerns you want to talk about.

Sincerely,
Tim Young

Tim Young

www.ingramcontent.com/pod-product-compliance
Lightning Source LLC
Chambersburg PA
CBHW040905180526
45159CB00010BA/2940